DR. PARESH B. ACHARYA

Educational Measurement and Evaluation

CANADIAN
Academic Publishing

2015

Educational Measurement and Evaluation

Dr. Paresh B. Acharya

M.Sc. (Maths), M.Ed., M.Phil., Ph.D., NET.

Assistant professor
Shri I. J. Patel M. Ed. Course
Mogri, Anand, India

CANADIAN
Academic Publishing

2015

Price : $27.86

First Edition : 2015

ISBN : 978-1-926488-22-6

ISBN Allotment Agency : Library and Archives Canada (Govt. of Canada)

Published & Printed by
Canadian Academic Publishing
81, Woodlot Crescent,
Etobicoke,
Toronto, Ontario, Canada.
Postal Code- M9W 6T3
http://www.canadapublish.com

PREFACE

Measurement and evaluation is a required subject in all teacher education sources. Its importance as a subject cannot be overemphasized for, with it, the teacher becomes empowered to assess the student's performance and assist them in learning process. We have tried to introduce this subject matter in this book in the simplest possible way in order to ensure that over would-be teachers will get the correct concepts and practices in educational measurement and evaluation.

The book consists seven chapters. The first chapter deals with basic concept of educational measurement and evaluations. The second chapter entitled 'taxonomy of educational objectives. The third chapter presents scales of measurement and types of tests. This book also takes a fresh look at accepted assessment concepts and issues, such as validity and reliabilities it presents in chapter four. Chapter five relate with evaluation of teaching learning process. Chapter six contains with statistical concepts essential for understanding the interpretation and discussion of result. using the results of measurement and evaluation including in the   last chapter of this book.

I hope this book equally beneficial for teachers of today and as well as, teachers of tomorrows.

- Dr. Paresh B. Acharya

CONTENTS

CHAPTER - 1
EDUCATIONAL MEASUREMENT AND EVALUATION

Educational measurement refers to the use of educational assessments and the analysis of data such as scores obtained from educational assessments to infer the abilities and proficiencies of students. The approaches overlap with those in psychometrics. Educational measurement is the assigning of numerals to traits such as achievement, interest, attitudes, aptitudes, intelligence and performance.

The aim of theory and practice in educational measurement is typically to measure abilities and levels of attainment by students in areas such as reading, writing, mathematics, science and so forth. Traditionally, attention focuses on whether assessments are reliable and valid. In practice, educational measurement is largely concerned with the analysis of data from educational assessments or tests. Typically, this means using total scores on assessments, whether they are multiple choice or open-ended and marked using marking rubrics or guides.

In technical terms, the pattern of scores by individual students to individual items is used to infer so-called scale locations of students, the "measurements". This process is one form of scaling. Essentially, higher total scores give higher scale locations, consistent with the traditional and everyday use of total scores. If certain theory is used, though; there is not a strict correspondence between the ordering of total scores and the ordering of scale locations. The Rasch model provides a strict correspondence provided all students attempt the same test items, or their performances are marked using the same marking rubrics.

In terms of the broad body of purely mathematical theory drawn on, there is substantial overlap between educational measurement and psychometrics. However, certain approaches considered to be a part of psychometrics, including Classical test theory, Item Response Theory and the Rasch model, were originally developed more specifically for the analysis of data from educational assessments.

One of the aims of applying theory and techniques in educational measurement is to try to place the results of different tests administered to different groups of students on a single or common scale through processes known as test equating. The rationale is that because different assessments usually have different difficulties, the total scores cannot be directly compared. The aim of trying to place results on a common scale is to allow comparison of the scale locations inferred from the totals via scaling processes.

Concept of Measurement

The process of measurement as it implies involves carrying out actual measurement in order to assign a quantitative meaning to a quality i.e. what is the length of the chalkboard? Determining this must be physically done. Measurement is therefore a process of assigning numerals to objects, quantities or events in other to give quantitative meaning to such qualities. In the classroom, to determine a child's performance, you need to obtain quantitative measures on the individual scores of the child. If the child scores 80 in Mathematics, there is no other interpretation you should give it. You cannot say he has passed or failed.

Educational evaluation is the evaluation process of characterizing and appraising some aspect/s of an educational process.

There are two common purposes in educational evaluation which are, at times, in conflict with one another. Educational institutions usually require evaluation data to demonstrate effectiveness to funders and other stakeholders, and to provide a measure of performance for marketing purposes. Educational evaluation is also a professional activity that individual educators need to undertake if they intend to continuously review and enhance the learning they are endeavoring to facilitate.

Teaching for successful learning cannot occur without high quality evaluation. Evaluation, therefore, needs to be integrated with the process of teaching and learning. The greater the integration the better the outcomes of learning. Hence, evaluation has to be so designed that it can be used as a powerful means of influencing the quality of what teachers teach and what students learn. But, while doing so special care must be taken to ensure that it is humane and it enables the learner to grow into a responsible and productive citizen. Not only this, evaluation has also to provide constant feedback regarding the effectiveness of course-contents, classroom processes and the growth of individual learners besides the appropriateness of the evaluation procedures. It must, however, be flexible enough to the extent that it can be experimented with and adapted according to the specific situations and needs of the learner groups. Evaluation is a systematic process of collecting, analyzing and interpreting evidences of students' progress and achievement both in cognitive and non-cognitive areas of learning for the purpose of taking a variety of decisions. Evaluation, thus, involves gathering and processing of information and decision-making.

Concept of Evaluation

Evaluation has a wider meaning. It goes beyond measurement. When from useful information including measurement, we make judgments, which are evaluation. Example: - The teacher may evaluate the student jaya that she is doing well in mathematics, because most of the class scored 50/100. This is an example of evaluation using quantitative data (measurable information). The teacher might also make an evaluation based on qualitative data, such as her observations that jaya works hard, has an enthusiastic attitude towards mathematics and finishes her assignments quickly.

Evaluation is a Science of providing information for decision making.

It Includes measurement, assessment and testing

It is a process that involves

Information gathering

Information processing

Judgment forming

Decision making

From the above, we can arrive at the following concept of evaluation

Evaluation is a concept that has emerged as a prominent process of assessing, testing and measuring. Its main objective is Qualitative Improvement.

Evaluation is a process of making value judgments over a level of performance or achievement. Making value judgments in Evaluation process presupposes the set of objectives

Evaluation implies a critical assessment of educative process and its outcome in the light of the objectives.

Principles of evaluation: evaluation should be,

Based on clearly stated objectives

Comprehensive

Cooperative

Used judiciously

Continuous and integral part of the teaching-learning process

Evaluation Process: As mentioned before, there are mainly three steps involved in evaluation process, i.e., aim, learning experience and tools of evaluation. Some consider modification of behavior as third step. All these steps are interlinked with each other.

Identifying and defining objectives

The aim is determined keeping in mind the social situation of the child, nature of contents and education level. Aim can successfully be determined in the form of behavior modification only when these points are kept in mind. Evaluator must know it vividly that to what extent behavior is to be changed. This will help in knowing whether the desired change is obtained or not. Thus, evaluation can only progress if the aims are properly

5

identified and defined. The content and behavior change should be given equal importance in defining the aims.

Planning the learning experience

Once the aims are identified and determined, the attention should be given to learning experience. Learning experience means creating such situation in which child can do the desired activities, i.e., is he may act according to aims,

Providing evidence through various tools of evaluation

After planning the learning experience the evaluator should select the proper tools. He should collect the evidences by using these tools. On the basis of this information he should evaluate the change in behavior.

Areas of change in behavior

The change in the behavior of a child is due to evaluation. Evaluation works as a means to these changes. The behaviour change can mainly be divided into three aspects:

Cognitive aspect

This aspect gives importance to cognition and knowledge. Bloom in his taxonomy included following aspects under this aspect:

Knowledge of subject related facts.

Knowledge of methods for obtaining special facts

Knowledge of traditions and values.

Knowledge of principles and generalizations.

Knowledge of criteria.

Knowledge of events.

Knowledge of methods and process.

Affective aspect
To accept.
To respond.
Evaluation.
Thinking
Organization
Characterization
Creative aspect
This is generally related to motor and limb movement.
This training programme can be divided into six levels:
Stimulus, Operation, Control, and Adjustment,
Temperamentalization, Proficiency
There is always coordination in these
aspects of behavior. The evaluation of these three aspects
can be done separately or in coordinate way.
Scope of evaluation
Related to the students
To determine the objectives
To select a particular group
Classification of the students
To select appropriate learning situation
To motivate the students
To develop ability and skill of the students
To find out the rate of improvement or progress
To predict future performance
 For grading purpose
 To diagnose the learning problem
Related to the teachers
To determine the effectiveness of teaching (teaching
        methods)
To adjust the content of course (in relation to determine
        the no. of subject and content of the syllabi)

Development of norms which may involve in evaluation
To conduct intensive research
To predict the performance and
To develop new programs in the field of teacher
    education.

Related to the curriculum/administration
Evaluating the curriculum program
Justify teacher education programs at different levels
Continuous assessment
Develop community interest
Develop and modification of instructional process
Overall assessment of total school/college program
Assessment of teacher's performance in all respect
Selection of teachers in various fields
    The following are the **functions of measurement
and evaluation in improving instruction**.
    Evaluation results enable the teacher to
accumulate the experiences and to follow-up diagnosed
results. The weaknesses of the pupils in the class can be
identified and remedied, thus pupils' performance is
enhanced.
    Measurement and evaluation measure pupils'
achievement and motivate pupils' learning. Pupils have
the right to know the progress they are making whether
they have attained the objectives of the subject matter or
not, thus results must be made known to them. It can also
encourage pupils to study more. They will be motivated
to participate actively in class and exert all efforts just to
make certain that they pass. They will know the quality
and amount of work they have to strive for.

Measurement and evaluation predict pupils' success and diagnoses pupils' difficulty. The success and failure of a pupil in the class can be predicted through it. The area where pupils excel must be enhanced or strengthened and where pupils fail should be remedied. The difficulties of the pupils should be given the priority for remediation. Knowing the successes and difficulties of the pupils, the teacher will be able to focus on the spots that need enhancement or remediation.

It is hope that evaluation results serve as the basis for the teacher to use appropriate teaching strategies and techniques that will improve instruction and provide the necessary learning for a pupil to acquire the knowledge and skills he needs.

CHAPTER - 2
TAXONOMY OF EDUCATIONAL OBJECTIVES

Bloom's Taxonomy

Bloom's taxonomy is a classification system used to define and distinguish different levels of human cognition—i.e., thinking, learning, and understanding. Educators have typically used Bloom's taxonomy to inform or guide the development of assessments (tests and other evaluations of student learning), curriculum (units, lessons, projects, and other learning activities), and instructional methods such as questioning strategies.

A Description of Bloom's Taxonomy and its Significance: Educational objectives indicate what students should attend to and put effort into learning; they are "explicit formulations of the ways in which students are expected to be changed by the educative process" (Bloom, 1956, p. 26). Bloom's taxonomy provides a well-accepted pedagogical framework for classifying vast numbers of educational objectives into useful structures. Benjamin Bloom's pioneering work on learning was initiated in 1948, when he headed a team of educators and psychologists investigating three major learning domains: cognitive, affective, and psychomotor. Over the last half-century, the theoretical framework produced by this team has facilitated analyses of learning objectives classification, criteria for performance-based learning, and levels of mastery in learning (Simon, 2000). To the extent that the goal of education is the diffusion of knowledge through learning, a description of Bloom's taxonomy represents a seminal work in developing and implementing high quality instruction.

10

Educational Taxonomies with examples, example questions and example activities.

Cognitive Domain :(Bloom)

1. KNOWLEDGE: Knowledge is defined as the remembering of previously learned material. This may involve the recall of a wide range of materials, from specific facts to complete theories, but all that is required is the bringing to mind of the appropriate information. Knowledge represents the lowest level of learning outcomes in the cognitive domain.

Description (to know   to recall):

- Remembering previously learned material
- Lowest level of learning
- Listing learned information
- Remembering terms, methods, facts, concepts, specific items of information

Sample Activities:

- Label the parts of a plant.
- Group together all the four syllable words.
- List the freedoms included in the Bill of Rights.
- Identify the food group to which each of these foods belongs.
- Write definitions to the following words.
- Locate examples of capitalization in the following story.
- Remember an idea or fact in somewhat the same form in which it was learned
- Question and answer sessions
- Workbooks/worksheets
- Programmed instruction
- Remember things read, heard, saw
- Games

- Information searches
- Reading assignments
- Drill and practice
- Finding definitions
- Memory games
- Quizzes
- Questions have right and wrong answers

Question/Statement Verbs:

*** Words alone may not ensure the desired level.

Choose, copy, define, describe, find, group, identify, indicate, label, list, locate, match, name, pick, point to, quote, recall, recite, select, sort, state, tell, underline, write, what, when, who

2. COMPREHENSION: Comprehension is defined as the ability to grasp the meaning of material. This may be shown by translating material from one form to another (words or numbers), by interpreting material (explaining or summarizing), and by estimating future trends (predicting consequences or effects). These learning outcomes go one step beyond the simple remembering of material, and represent the lowest level of understanding.

Description (explaining and understanding):
- Ability to grasp the meaning of material
- Communicating an idea
- Explaining ideas
- Summarizing material
- Understanding facts and principles

Sample Activities:

Give reasons for the energy crisis.

Explain why we have bus safety rules.

Outline the steps necessary for an idea to become a law.

Restate the reasons for weather changes.

Summarize the story.
What were the underlying factors that contributed to the Revolutionary War?
Communicate an idea
Giving examples of
Paraphrasing
Peer teaching
Show and tell
Give reasons for
Question/Statement Verbs:
Compare, comprehend, conclude, contrast, demonstrate, explain, expound, illustrate, outline, predict, rephrase

3. APPLICATION: Application refers to the ability to use learned material in new and concrete situations. This may include the application of such things as rules, methods, concepts, principles, laws, and theories. Learning outcomes in this area require a higher level of understanding than those under comprehension.

Description (using ideas):
Applying concepts and principles to new situations
Applying laws and theories to practical situations
Solving of mathematical problems
Constructing charts and graphs
Demonstrating correct usage of a method or procedure
Applying rules, methods, concepts, principles, laws, theories
Requires higher level of understanding than comprehension

Sample Activities:
• Put this information in graph form.
• Organize the forms of pollution from most damaging to least damaging.

- Sketch a picture that relates your feelings of recess.
- Using knowledge from various areas to find solutions to problems
- Applying ideas to new or unusual situations
- Simulation Activities
- Role playing/role reversal
- Model building
- Interviewing
- Group presentation
- Conducting experiments
- Practical applications of learned knowledge
- Suggest actual uses of ideas

Question/Statement Verbs:

Apply, construct, classify, develop, organize, solve, test, use, utilize, wield

4. ANALYSIS: Analysis refers to the ability to break down material into its component parts so that its organizational structure may be understood. This may include the identification of the parts, analysis of the relationships between parts, and the recognition of the organizational principles involved. Learning outcomes here represent a higher intellectual level than comprehension and application because they require an understanding of both the content and the structural form of the material.

Description (breaking down):

- Breaking material down into component parts
- Understanding the organizational structure
- Analysis of relationships between parts
- Recognition of organizational principles involved

- Understanding both the content and structural form
- Analyzing the elements
  Sample Activities:
- Simplify the ballet to its basic moves and.
- Inspect a house for poor workmanship and
- Observe a painting to uncover as many principles of art as possible and
- Read a nonfiction book. Divide the book into its parts. Tell why the parts were placed in the order they were.
- Look into the forces that might cause pressure for our legislators and
- Inspect two presidential speeches. Compare and contrast them in writing.
- Uncovering unique characteristics
- Distinguishing between facts and inferences
- Evaluating the relevancy of data
- Recognizing logical fallacies in reasoning
- Recognizing unstated assumptions
- Analyzing the organizational structure of a work (of art, music, or writing)
- Comparing and contrasting
- Problem identification
- Attribute listing
- Morphological analysis

Question/Statement Verbs:
analyze, assume, breakdown, classify, compare, contrast, discriminate, dissect, distinguish, divide, deduce, diagram, examine, inspect, infer, reason, recognize, separate, simplify, section, scrutinize, survey, search, study, screen, sift, subdivide, take apart

5. SYNTHESIS: Synthesis refers to the ability to put parts together to form a new whole. This may involve the production of a unique communication (theme or speech), a plan of operations (research proposal), or a set of abstract relations (scheme for classifying information). Learning outcomes in this area stress creative behaviors, with major emphasis on the formulation of new patterns or structures.

Description (forming new whole):
- Putting parts together in a new whole
- Formulating new patterns or structures
- Abstract relationships
- Communicating an idea in a unique way
- Proposing a new set of operations
- Creating new or original things
- Take things and pattern them in a new way

Sample Activities:
- Create a new song for the melody of "Mary Had a Little Lamb."
- Combine elements of drama, music, and dance into a stage presentation.
- Develop a plan for your school to save money.
- Create a model of a new game that combines thinking, memory, and chance equally.
- Reorganize a chapter/unit from your textbook the way you think it should be.
- Find an unusual way to communicate the story of a book you have read.
- Formulate positive changes that would improve learning in your classroom.
- Develop an original plan
- Writing a well organized theme

- Writing a creative story, poem, or song
- Proposing a plan for an experiment
- Integrating the learning from different areas into a plan for solving a problem
- Formulating a new scheme for classifying objects
- Finding new combinations
- Showing how an idea or product might be changed

Question/Statement Verbs:

build, create, combine, compile, compose, construct, develop, design, derive, form, formulate, generate, how, make, make up, modify, produce, plan, propose, reorder, reorganize, rearrange, reconstruct, revise, suggest, synthesize, what, write

6. EVALUATION: Evaluation is concerned with the ability to judge the value of material (statement, novel, poem, research report) for a given purpose. The judgments are to be based on definite criteria. These may be internal criteria (organization) or external criteria (relevance to the purpose) and the student may determine the criteria or be given them. Learning outcomes in this area are highest in the cognitive hierarchy because they contain elements of all of the other categories, plus value judgments based on clearly defined criteria.

Description (judging):
- Ability to judge the value of material
- Use of definite criteria for judgments
- Value judgments based on clearly defined criteria
- Use of cognitive and affective thinking together

Sample Activities:
- Decide which person would best fill a position.

- Rank the principles of "good sportsmanship" in order of importance to you.
- Decide which proposed plan is the best.
- Read two different accounts of an incident. Decide which story is most logical in its portrayal.
- Judge the posters or murals your class has just constructed.
- Justify the actions of your favorite historical figure.
- Determine the necessary criteria for a good resource.
- Summarize the involvements you have had with your class this year.
- Making judgments about data or ideas based on either internal or external conditions or criteria
- Rating ideas
- Accepting or rejecting ideas based on standards
- Judging the logical consistency of written material
- Judging the adequacy with which conclusions are supported with data
- Judging the value of a work (of art, music, writing) by using internal criteria or external standards of excellence
- Generating criteria for evaluation
- Making evaluations for peer projects and presentations
- Evaluating one's own products and ideas

Question/Statement Verbs:

appraise, accept/reject, assess, check, choose, conclude, criticize, decide, defend, determine, discriminate, evaluate, interpret, justify, judge, prioritize, rate, rank, reject/accept, referee, select, settle, support, umpire, weigh, which,

Affective Domain: (Bloom and Krathwohl)

1. RECEIVING: refers to the student's willingness to attend to particular phenomena or stimuli (classroom activities, textbook, music, etc.). From a teaching standpoint, it is concerned with getting, holding, and directing the student's attention. Learning outcomes in this area range from the simple awareness that a thing exists to selective attention on the part of the learner. Receiving represents the lowest level of learning outcomes in the affective domain.

Descriptive Activities:
•   Listens attentively
•   Shows awareness of the importance of learning
•   Shows sensitivity to social problems
•   Accepts differences of race and culture
•   Attends closely to the classroom activities

Question/Statement Verbs:

Asks, chooses, describes, follows, gives, holds, identifies, locates, names, points to, selects, sits erect, replies,

2. RESPONDING: refers to active participation on the part of the student. At this level he not only attends to a particular phenomenon but also reacts to it in some way. Learning outcomes in this area may emphasize acquiescence in responding (reads beyond assignments) or satisfaction in responding (reads for pleasure or enjoyment). The higher levels of this category include those instructional objectives that are commonly classified under interest; that is, those that stress the seeking out and enjoyment of particular activities.

Descriptive Activities:

- Completes assigned homework
- Obeys school rules
- Participates in class discussion
- Completes laboratory work
- Volunteers for special tasks
- Shows interest in the subject
- Enjoys helping others

Question/Statement Verbs:

Answers, assists, complies, conforms, discusses, greets, helps, labels, performs, practices, presents, reads, recites, tells, reports, selects, writes

3. VALUING: is concerned with the worth or value a student attaches to a particular object, phenomenon, or behavior. This ranges in degree from the simpler acceptance of a value (desires to improve group skills) to the more complex level of commitment (assumes responsibility for the effective functioning of the group). Valuing is based on the internalization of a set of specified values, but clues to these values are expressed in the student's overt behavior that is consistent and stable enough to make the value clearly identifiable. Instructional objectives that are commonly classified under attitudes and appreciation would fall into this category.

Descriptive Activities:

- Demonstrates belief in the democratic process
- Appreciates good literature
- Appreciates the role of science in everyday life
- Shows concern for the welfare of others

- Demonstrates problem solving attitude
- Demonstrates commitment to social improvement

Question/Statement Verbs:

Completes, describes, differentiates, explains, follows, forms, initiates, invites, joins, justifies, proposes, reads, reports, selects, shares, studies, works

4. ORGANIZATION: is concerned with bringing together values, resolving conflicts between them, and beginning the building of an internally consistent value system. Thus the emphasis is on comparing, relating, and synthesizing values. Learning outcomes may be concerned with the conceptualization of a value (recognizes the responsibility of each individual for improving human relations) or with the organization of a value system (develops a vocational plan that satisfies his need for both economic security and social service). Instructional objectives relating to the development of a philosophy of life would fall into this category.

Descriptive Activities:

- Recognizes the need for balance between freedom and responsibility in a democracy
- Recognizes the role of systematic planning in problem solving
- Accepts responsibility for own behavior
- Understands and accepts own strengths and weaknesses
- Formulates a life plan in harmony with his abilities, interests, and beliefs

Question/Statement Verbs:

Adheres, alters, arranges, combines, compares, completes, defends, explains, generalizes, identifies, integrates, modifies, orders, organizes, prepares, relates, synthesizes

5. CHARACTERIZATION BY A VALUE OR VALUE COMPLEX: at this level of the affective domain, the individual has a value system that has controlled his behavior for a sufficiently long time for him to develop a characteristic life style. Thus the behavior is pervasive, consistent, and predictable. Learning outcomes at this level cover a broad range of activities, but the major emphasis is on the fact that the behavior is typical or characteristic of the student. Instructional objectives that are concerned with the student's general patterns of adjustment (personal, social, emotional) would be appropriate here.

Descriptive Activities:

- Displays safety consciousness
- Demonstrates self reliance in working independently
- Practices cooperation in-group activities
- Uses objective approach in problem solving
- Demonstrates industry and self discipline
- Maintains good health habits

Question/Statement Verbs:

Acts, discriminates, displays, influences, listens, modifies, per forms, practices, pro poses, qualifies, questions, revises, serves, solves, uses, verifies

Psychomotor Domain: (Bloom and Harrow)

1. PERCEPTION: the first level is concerned with the use of the sense organs to obtain cues that guide motor activity. This category ranges from sensory stimulation (awareness of a stimulus), through cue selection

(selection task relevant cues) to translation (relating cue perception to action in performance).

Descriptive Activities:
- Recognizes malfunction by sound of machine
- Relates taste of food to need for seasoning
- Relates music to a particular dance movement

Question/Statement Verbs:

Chooses, describes, detects, differentiates, distinguishes, identifies, isolates, relates, selects, separates

2. SET: refers to readiness to take a particular type of action. This category includes mental set (mental readiness to act), physical set (physical readiness to act), and emotional set (willingness to act). Perception of cues serves as an important prerequisite for this level.

Descriptive Activities:
- Knows mechanical sequence of steps in varnishing wood
- Demonstrates proper bodily stance for batting a ball
- Show desire to type efficiently by placement of hands and body

Question/Statement Verbs:

Begins, displays, explains, moves, proceeds, reacts, responds, shows, starts, volunteers

3. GUIDED RESPONSE: is concerned with the early stages in learning a complex skill. It includes imitation (repeating an act demonstrated by the instructor) and trial and error (using a multiple response approach to identify an appropriate response). Adequacy of performance is judged by an instructor or by a suitable set of criteria.

Descriptive Activities:

- Performs a golf swing as demonstrated
- Applies first aid bandage as demonstrated
- Determines best physical manipulation of objects in a sequence for preparing a meal

Question/Statement Verbs:

Assembles, builds, calibrates, constructs, dismantles, displays, dissects, fastens, fixes, grinds, heats, manipulates, measures, mends, organizes, sketches

4. MECHANISM: is concerned with performance acts where the learned responses have become habitual and the movements can be performed with some confidence and proficiency. Learning outcomes at this level are concerned with performance skills of various types, but the movement patterns are less complex than at the next higher level.

Descriptive Activities:
- Writes smoothly and legibly
- Sets up laboratory equipment
- Operates a slide projector
- Demonstrates a simple dance step

Question/Statement Verbs:

(Same list as for guided response)

5. COMPLEX OVERT RESPONSE: is concerned with the skillful performance of motor acts that involve complex movement patterns. Proficiency is indicated by a quick, smooth, accurate performance, requiring a minimum of energy. The category includes resolution of uncertainty (performs without hesitation) and automatic performance (movements are made with ease and good muscle control). Learning outcomes at this level include highly coordinated motor activities.

Descriptive Activities:

- Operates a power saw skillfully
- Demonstrates correct form in swimming
- Demonstrates skill in driving an automobile
- Performs skillfully on the violin
- Repairs electronic equipment quickly and accurately

Question/Statement Verbs:

(Same list as for guided response)

6. ADAPTATION: is concerned with skills that are so well developed that the individual can modify movement patterns to fit special requirements or to meet a problem situation.

Descriptive Activities:

- Adjusts tennis play to counteract opponent's style
- Modifies swimming strokes to fit the roughness of the water

Question/Statement Verbs:

Adapts, alters, changes, rearranges, reorganizes, revises, varies

7. ORIGINATION: refers to the creating of a new movement pattern to fit a particular situation or specific problem. Learning outcomes at this level emphasize creativity based upon highly developed skills.

Descriptive Activities:

- Creates a dance step
- Creates a musical composition
- Designs a new dress style

Question/Statement Verbs:

Arranges, combines, composes, constructs, creates, designs, originates

Revised taxonomy

One of Bloom's former students led a diverse group of researchers to update Bloom's original taxonomy of learning. The result of this group's work, a revised taxonomy of learning, was published in 2001. The revised taxonomy is different from the original taxonomy in several ways. The most significant change is the use of a two-dimensional model that addresses both what is being learned and how that knowledge is being learned, rather than just a one-dimensional linear description of learning (Forehand, 2005). In addition to the change in the number of dimensions, the revised model has some renamed dimensions and uses verbs to describe the levels of learning instead of nouns. The categories of the revised taxonomy are remembering, understanding, applying, analyzing, evaluating, and creating. These categories are used to describe the cognitive process (Cruz, 2003). This revised taxonomy models the interaction between these subcategories (which describe the cognitive process) and different dimensions of knowledge (factual knowledge, conceptual knowledge, procedural knowledge, and metacognitive knowledge) (Cruz, 2003). This model allows for a description of what is being learned (type of knowledge) and how it is being learned (the procedural level).

Strengths & Weaknesses

Bloom's taxonomy can and has been applied to many different learning environments and situations for a variety of purposes (i.e. designing assessments, designing coursework, designing curricula, etc.) (Forehand, 2005).

Bloom's taxonomy is relatively easy to understand (Forehand, 2005; Kottke & Schuster, 1990).This taxonomy is widely accepted and and often referenced in the field of education (Forehand, 2005; Kottke & Schuster, 1990; Kunen et al., 1981). It has been translated and used in many countries (Forehand, 2005), which is a good demonstration of the extent of its use. Because it is widely used and accepted, these taxonomies provide a common language for the discussion of many topics in education. The results of most empirical studies of the underlying assumptions of these models have been inconclusive (Hill & McGraw, 1981; Kottke & Schuster, 1990; Kunen, Cohen, & Solomon, 1981). Empirical research has not consistently supported many of the assumptions which have become widely accepted. Despite widespread use of Bloom's taxonomy for identifying the types and/or difficulty of test questions, validity for use of this taxonomy for creating test questions has not been established (Blumberg, Alschuler, & Rezmovia, 1982; Kottke & Schuster, 1990).

Models of Educational Evaluation

Alexander and Hedberg (1994) summarize the representative approaches used in educational research over the past 50 year and give the following four key paradigms with their perceived advantages and disadvantages:

Objective-based: Evaluation as a process of determining the degree to which educational objectives are being achieved. This follows the scientific tradition and is straightforward to apply, but does not take account of unintended outcomes, and takes no account of students as individuals with all their differences.

Decision-based: Focuses on the decisions made during development and improvements that could be made. It is useful for programs with a large scope or multiple levels, but needs the co-operation of decision makers. It has proved difficult to put into practice and expensive to maintain.

Value-based: Evaluation is not only concerned with goals, but also whether the goals are worth achieving. Formative and summative evaluation is used, and the evaluator considers major effects, achievements and consequences of the program. This acknowledges the importance of unintended outcomes, and learners' perceptions of the learning experience, and evaluation can be made without the need to know about the objectives. Its perceived disadvantages are that it may leave important questions unanswered.

Naturalistic approach: organizes evaluations around the participants' key concerns and issues. Uses qualitative data collection such as journals, observations and interview. The advantages are that it acknowledges context and can be used to benefit those being studied, but participants may identify criteria with little educational worth.

CHAPTER - 3
SCALES OF MEASUREMENT
AND TYPE OF TEST

Scales of Measurement

It is clear that educational measurement can seldom be done at the same level as physical measurement. The goal should be to measure as precisely as possible approaching the accuracy of physical measurements. But due to practical limitations, sometimes the best can be done in education is the mere ordering or ranking of individuals.

Still we can develop a consistent scheme for classifying measurement scales according to different level of refinement. It is generally agreed that there are four kinds of measurement scales according to corresponding levels of measurement. A mention of these four scales has been made earlier also, but there is need to discuss them in detail:

Nominal or Classificatory scale

Ordinal or Ranking scale

Interval Scale

Ration scale

Nominal or Classificatory scale

The nominal scale represents the lowest level of refinement. Some may even question whether this level of measurement is measurement at all. In this scale the set of objects are distributed among unordered categories on the basis of qualitative differences among the objects. Numbers or other symbols are used simply to classify an object, person, and characteristic or to identify the groups to which various objects belong. For example, psychiatric grouping of persons is a nominal scale. In this system, the diagnostician classifies persons into various groups such as schizophrenic, paranoid, manic-depressive, etc. Classification of persons into males and females, into rural and urban categories, into various communities and castes are some other examples. Numbers of vehicles is another such scale, because automobiles are classified into various sub-classes, each indicating a district or region. The numbers assigned do not indicate even any order. They are used only to name, identify or classify. Giving roll numbers to students or numbers to players illustrate this limited significance of numbers. The only permissible arithmetical operations in their case are counting and statistical techniques based on counting.

In a normal scale, a given class is subdivided into set of mutually exclusive subclasses. Members of a subclass are equivalent in respect of the property being measured. A one to one transformation exists in this scale, i.e., symbols designating various groups may be interchanged without altering essential information provided by the scale.

Ordinal or Ranking scale

When the observations are ordered in such a way we can call an observation superior to another in respect of the given variable, then it is an example of an ordinal scale. In this scale, each of a set of objects is assigned on the basis of certain rules, to one of a set of ordered categories. These categories are assigned in order according to the amount of a trait or characteristics. The categories differ quantitatively from one another. For example, we categories each pupil in a class as(i) above average, (ii) average or (iii) below average on the basis of reading ability.

The social classes in a country-lower, lower middle, upper middle and upper-constitute an ordinal scale. In such a classification, each class is higher than the classes below it, and lower than the classes above it. When students are asked to stand in a row from the tallest to the shortest, it will also constitute an ordinal scale. The numbers used in identifying our observations are called ranks.

The fundamental difference between a nominal and an ordinal scale is that the nominal scale incorporates the relation of equivalence only, whereas ordinal scale incorporates the relation of equivalence as well as of 'greater than.'

Ranks do tell that one observation represents more or less of the variable than another, but they do not tell us how much more or less. The ranks or successive intervals (distances between classes) on the scales are not equal. Therefore ordinal scale cannot be subjected to arithmetical calculations. There is neither an absolute zero nor are the units of measurements uniform throughout. The categories help only in ranking or ordering. The only permissible arithmetical operation is that of ranking, and statistical techniques based on ranking. Accordingly, an ordinal scale is useful when it possible to express a characteristics quantitatively but impossible to define units of measurement which are equal at all points on the scale. Most of measurements in education can be done at the level of ordinal scales, unless we make assumptions about the uniformity of units.

Interval scale

The interval scale also involves quantification, but with an added refinement, viz, the differences between consecutive points on the scale are equal over the entire scale. Of course, there is no absolute zero. All that it implies is that there are uniform units. The numbers used represent not only an ordering of the observation but also convey meaningful information with respect to the distance or degree of difference between all observations.

The arithmetical operations of multiplication and division are not permitted at this level of measurement. However, addition and subtraction as also the statistical techniques based on them are permitted. Means, Standard Deviations and Correlations can be applied to the data obtained in an interval scale.

Measurement of temperature is an example of such a scale. Here the difference between 39° and 40° is exactly equal to that between 55° and 56° or between any two adjacent points on the scale. But in the interval scale, we cannot say that a value of 100 is twice as great as the value of 50.

Most scales used for measuring cognitive characteristics in education are assumed to be interval scales, although this assumption is sometimes a violation. It is assumed, for example, that the difference between scores of 50 and 53 on an achievement test is equivalent to the difference between scores of 20 and 23 on the same test. While this may be entirely true only under certain very specific conditions, i.e. when item-difficulty levels and measurement errors are strictly controlled, it is not a reasonable assumption for some tests in current use in education.

Ratio scale

The ratio scales represent the most refined level of measurement as they have a defined zero point and uniform units of measurement. When a scale has all the characteristics of an interval scale, and in addition has a true zero-point as its origin it is named as a ratio scale. In this scale, the ratio of any two scale points is independent of the unit of measurement. Each number, that we assign, can be thought of as a distance measured from zero. There are no limitations as far as the use of arithmetical operations or statistical techniques are concerned. Many of the physical measurements are done at this level.

Measurement of length and weight are examples of such a scale. If a person's height is 80 cm, it can be said with certainty that he is twice as tall as one whose height is only 40 cm. The concept of zero height is a definable concept.

On the other hand, an individual who has an IQ of 120 is not twice as intelligent as one who has an IQ of 60. The concept of zero intelligence is a meaningless concept just as is the concept of zero achievement as measured by a particular test. We cannot compare even the differences between the marks obtained because of a lack of uniformity of units. That is why we have not succeeded much in using ratio sales in psychological and educational measurements. Instead we have to depend upon ordinal scale in these measurements.

But we cannot ignore the advantages possessed by the ratio scales, which are:

1.   In this scale the data can be subjected to arithmetical operations like addition, subtraction, multiplication and division. These operations are permissible on the numerical values assigned to the objects as well as on the intervals between numerals.

2.   It has a true zero point; therefore it has the possibility to indicate the complete absence of characteristics.

3.   Among all the scales it is the most precise type of measurement.

Meaning of test:

-Test may be called as tool, a question, set of question, and an examination which use to measure a particular characteristic of an individual or a group of individuals.

-It is something which provides information regarding individual's ability, knowledge, performance and achievement.

Nature of test:

-The test is reliable

-The test is valid

- It is objective

-Must accomplish with norms

- Should not be expensive

-Less time consuming

-Must produce results and its implementation

-Its feasibility
-Must have educational values

Types of Tests

The nature of type of a test is determined by the particular purpose of measurement. Various authors have given different classification of tests. A number of categories in these classifications may appear to overlap. These classifications give a broad idea of the extensive field of testing.

Classifications of Tests

1. On the basis of type of questions
(a) Essay or Free Answer type
(b) Short Answer Type
(c) Objective or New Type
Which comprise,
(i) Alternative Response Type,
(ii) Multiple Response Type,
(iii) Matching Type,
(iv) Completion Type,
(v) Simple Recall Type,
2. On the basis of Administration
(a) Individual vs. Group tests
(b) Oral vs. Written tests
(c) Speed vs. Power tests
3. On the basis of standardization
(a) Non-standardized tests

(b)   Teacher-made Informal Objective tests

(c)   Standardized tests

4.   On the basis of scoring

(a)   Amenable to qualitative scoring

(b)   Amenable to stencil or punch board scoring

(c)   Amenable to machine scoring

5.   On the basis of Traits

(a)   Intelligence tests

(b)   Tests of Special Abilities

(c)   Personality Tests and Adjustment Inventories

Initial Evaluation Assessment Checklist

Who? (Target - know your audience)
        Who is the evaluation for?

What? (Area - understand what it is you are evaluating)
        -Process (Efficiency)
        -Outcome (Effectiveness)
        -Combination of both (Relevance)
        -Purpose (Validate, Improve or Condemn)

When? (Timing - don't start until you are ready)
        -have you defined a question?
        -will the findings have any effect?
        -benefits outweigh costs

How? (Techniques - what is most appropriate)
        -Questionnaires
        -Interviews
        -Confidence Logs
        -Observations
        -Student Profiles
        -Pre-Tests and Post Tests
        -Inventory Learning Checklists

Test construction:
It could be divided into three phases:
1. Planning the test
2. Item writing
3. Item analysis

When to Use Essay or Objective Tests
Essay tests are especially appropriate when:
- the group to be tested is small and the test is not to be reused.
- you wish to encourage and reward the development of student skill in writing.
- you are more interested in exploring the student's attitudes than in measuring his/her achievement.
- you are more confident of your ability as a critical and fair reader than as an imaginative writer of good objective test items.

   Objective tests are especially appropriate when:
- the group to be tested is large and the test may be reused.
- highly reliable test scores must be obtained as efficiently as possible.
- impartiality of evaluation, absolute fairness, and freedom from possible test scoring influences (e.g., fatigue, lack of anonymity) are essential.
- you are more confident of your ability to express objective test items clearly than of your ability to judge essay test answers correctly.
- there is more pressure for speedy reporting of scores than for speedy test preparation.

   Either essay or objective tests can be used to:

- measure almost any important educational achievement a written test can measure.
- test understanding and ability to apply principles.
- test ability to think critically.
- test ability to solve problems.
- test ability to select relevant facts and principles and to integrate them toward the solution of complex problems.

CHAPTER - 4
ITEM ANALYSIS, RELIABILITY AND VALIDITY

Meaning, Characteristics and Procedure

The characteristics of a good test have been discussed in the earlier chapters, but these characteristics are depending upon the characteristics of the items of a test. The validity is most important characteristic of measuring instruments which refers to the purposiveness of the test. The validity of a test depends on the validity of the test items. If the items have the high validity, then the test validity will also be high. After preparing objective type items which are subjected to the item analysis. Item analysis technique helps in selecting the best items for final draft of the test and poor items are rejected and some of the items are modified. In this chapter meaning of item analysis, indexes of items and procedure of item analysis have been discussed in detail.

Ross has enumerated four steps for the construction of an objective type test.

1. Planning of test
2. Preparing test
3. Trying out of test and
4. Evaluating test

Item analysis is done in the third step-tries out of test. In the second step items are prepared by test designer. These items are tried out to examine their characteristics. The main task in trying out is the item analysis. The trying out is of three types

(a) Individual tryout, or Preliminary tryout
(b) Group tryout, or proper try out and
(c) Final try out.

(a)   Preliminary Try out: The main purpose of it is try out is to improve and modify the language ambiguity and difficulty. The subjects are selected from the population for which the test is being designed. This try out is done individually to locate the item difficulty and ambiguity of language. The improvement is made in the destructors and the correct answer or best answer. The powerful destructor and poor destructors are changed. The following rules are observed in this try out. The preliminary draft of the test should be prepared on cards with pencil. The draft should include more items than the desirable items in final draft.

(1)   The items should be objective type in statement form.

(2)   All the items of same type should be placed together in the test.

(b) Proper try out: This type of try out is done on a group of students selected from the target population. After preliminary try out same printed or cyclostyled copies of the test are prepared. The main purpose of this try out is to take decision about items on the basis statistical method to be employed for obtaining items indexes:

(1)   Difficulty value and

(2)   Discriminative power

The scoring key can also be checked and can be, improved for the correct responses. The following are the sub-steps which are used in proper try out

1. Administration of the test, on a group students the size maybe at least 40 students.

2. Scoring the answer sheets of the subjects.

3. Analysis of destructors-powerful and poor destructors.

40

4. Guessing correction.

5. Item Analysis is done for obtaining

a. Difficulty value and

b. Discriminative power

Item Analysis

It is a statistical technique which- is used for selecting and rejecting the items of a test' on the basis of their difficulty value and discriminative power. Item analysis is concerned basically with the two characteristics of an item-difficulty value and discriminative power.

Need of Item Analysis

Item analysis is a technique by which the test items are selected and rejected. 'The selection of items may serve the purpose of the designer or test constructor, because the items have such characteristics. The following arc the main purpose of the tests

(a)   Classification of students or candidates.

(b)   Selection of the candidates for the job.

(c)   Gradation is an academic purpose to assign grades or divisions to the students

(d)   Prognosis and promotion of - the candidates or students.

(e)   Establishing individual differences, and

(f)   Research for the verification of hypotheses.

The different purposes require different types of test having the items of different characteristics. The selection or entrance test includes the items of high difficult value as well as high power of discrimination. The promotion or prognostic test has the items of moderate difficulty value. There are various techniques of item analysis which are used these days.

The Objectives of Item Analysis

The following are the main objectives of item analysis technique

(1)   The main objective of item analysis is to select the appropriate items for the final draft and reject the poor items which do not contribute in the functioning of the test. Some items are to be modified.

(2)   Item analysis obtains the difficulty values of all the items of preliminary .draft of the test. The items are classified-difficult, moderate and easy items.

(3)   It provides the discriminative power (item reliability/validity) to differentiate between capable and less capable examinees of all the items preliminary draft of the test. The items are classified on the basis of the indexes-positive, negative and no discrimination. 'File negative and no discrimination power items are rejected out rightly.

(4)   It also indicates the functioning of the destructors in the multiple-choice items. The powerful and poor destructors are changed. It provides the basis for the modification to be made in some of the items of preliminary draft.

(5)   The reliability and validity of test depends oil these characterizes of a test. The functioning of a test is increased by this technique. Both these indexes are considered simultaneously in selecting and rejecting the items of a test.

(6)   It provides the basis for preparing (lie final draft a test. In the final draft items are arranged in difficulty order. The most easy items are given in the beginning and most difficult items are provided at the end,

(7)   Item analysis is a cyclic technique. The modified items are tried out and their item analysis is done again to obtain these indexes (difficulty and discrimination). The empirical evidences are obtained for selecting the modified items for the final draft.

Functions of Item Analysis

The main function of item analysis is to obtain the indexes of the items which indicate its basic characteristics. There are three characteristics-

(1)   Item difficulty value (D.V.) is the proportion of subjects answering each item correctly.

(2)   Discriminative power (D.P.) of item, this characteristics is of two type

(a)   Item reliability it is taken as the point-biserial correlation between an item and the total test score, multiplied by the item standard deviation.

(b)   Item validity-it is taken as the point biserial correlation between an item and a criterion score multiplied by the item standard deviation.

The test as a whole should fulfill its purpose successfully, each of its items must be able to discriminate between high and poor students oil the test. In other words, a test fulfils its purpose with maximum success when each item serves as good predictor. Therefore it is essential that cacti item of the test should be analyzed in terms of its difficulty value and discriminative power for the justification. Item analysis serves the following purpose-

(1)   To improve and modify a test for immediate use on a parallel group of subjects.

(2)   To select the best items for a test with regard to its purpose after a proper try out on the group

of subjects selected from the target population.

(3) To provide the statistical check up for the characteristics of tile test items for the judgment of test designer.

(4) To set up parallel forms of a test. Parallel form of test should not require only having similar items content or type of items but they should also have the same difficulty value and discriminative power. Item analysis technique that exactly parallel test can be developed, provides the empirical basis.

(5) To modify and reject the. Poor items of the test. The poor items may not serve the purpose of the test. The powerful distracters of items are changed and poor distracters are also changed.

(6) Item analysis is usually done of a power test rather than speed test. It speed test all the items are of the same difficulty value. The purpose of speed test is to measure the speed and accuracy while speed is acquired through practice. There is no power test, because the time limit is imposed, therefore these are the speeded test. The speediness' of the test depends on the difficulty values of the items of the test. ? Most of the students should reach to last items, in the allotted time for the test.

Item analysis is the study of the statistical properties of test items. The qualities usually of interest arc the difficulty of the, item and its ability or power to differentiate between more capable and less capable examinees. Difficulty is usually expressed as the percent or proportion getting the item right, and discrimination as some index comparing success by the more capable and the less capable students.

Qualitative Item Analysis

Qualitative item analysis procedures include careful proofreading of the exam prior to its administration for typographical errors, for grammatical cues that might inadvertently tip off examinees to the correct answer, and for the appropriateness of the reading level of the material. Such procedures can also include small group discussions of the quality of the exam and its items with examinees who have already taken the test, or with departmental student assistants, or even experts in the field. Some faculty use a "think-aloud test administration" (cf. Cohen, Swerdlik, & Smith, 1992) in which examinees are asked to express verbally what they are thinking as they respond to each of the items on an exam. This procedure can assist the instructor in determining whether certain students (such as those who performed well or those who performed poorly on a previous exam) misinterpreted particular items, and it can help in determining *why* students may have misinterpreted a particular item.

Quantitative Item Analysis:

In addition to these and other qualitative procedures, a thorough item analysis also includes a number of quantitative procedures. Specifically, three numerical indicators are often derived during an item analysis: **item difficulty, item discrimination,** and **distracter power** statistics.

Item Difficulty Index (p):

The item difficulty statistic is an appropriate choice for achievement or aptitude tests when the items are scored dichotomously (i.e., correct vs. incorrect).

Thus, it can be derived for true-false, multiple-choice, and matching items, and even for essay items, where the instructor can convert the range of possible point values into the categories "passing" and "failing."

The item difficulty index, symbolized p, can be computed simply by dividing the number of test takers who answered the item correctly by the total number of students who answered the item. As a proportion, p can range between 0.00, obtained when no examinees answered the item correctly, and 1.00, obtained when all examinees answered the item correctly. Notice that no test item need have only one p value. Not only may the p value vary with each class group that takes the test, an instructor may gain insight by computing the item difficulty level for a number of different subgroups within a class, such as those who did well on the exam overall and those who performed more poorly. Although the computation of the item difficulty index p is quite straightforward, the interpretation of this statistic is not. To illustrate, consider an item with a difficulty level of 0.20. We do know that 20% of the examinees answered the item correctly, but we cannot be certain why they did so. Does this item difficulty level mean that the item was challenging for all but the best prepared of the examinees? Does it mean that the instructor failed in his or her attempt to teach the concept assessed by the item? Does it mean that the students failed to learn the material? Does it mean that the item was poorly written? To answer these questions, we must rely on other item analysis procedures, both qualitative and quantitative ones.

Item Discrimination Index (D):

Item discrimination analysis deals with the fact that often different test takers will answer a test item in different ways. As such, it addresses questions of considerable interest to most faculty, such as, "does the test item differentiate those who did well on the exam overall from those who did not?" or "does the test item differentiate those who know the material from those who do not?" In a more technical sense then, item discrimination analysis addresses the validity of the items on a test, that is, the extent to which the items tap the attributes they were intended to assess. As with item difficulty, item discrimination analysis involves a family of techniques. Which one to use depends on the type of testing situation and the nature of the items. I'm going to look at only one of those, the item discrimination index, symbolized D. The index parallels the difficulty index in that it can be used wherever items can be scored dichotomously, as correct or incorrect, and hence it is most appropriate for true-false, multiple-choice, and matching items, and for those essay items which the instructor can score as "pass" or "fail."

We test because we want to find out if students know the material, but all we learn for certain is how they did on the exam we gave them. The item discrimination index tests the test in the hope of keeping the correlation between knowledge and exam performance as close as it can be in an admittedly imperfect system.

The item discrimination index is calculated in the following way:

1.   Divide the group of test takers into two groups, high scoring and low scoring. Ordinarily, this is done by dividing the examinees into those scoring above and those scoring below the median. (Alternatively, one could create groups made up of the top and bottom quintiles or quartiles or even deciles.)

2.   Compute the item difficulty levels separately for the upper (p upper) and lower (p lower) scoring groups.

3.   Subtract the two difficulty levels such that $D = p$ upper- power.

How is the item discrimination index interpreted? Unlike the item difficulty level p, the item discrimination index can take on negative values and can range between -1.00 and 1.00. Consider the following situation: suppose that overall, half of the examinees answered a particular item correctly, and that all of the examinees who scored above the median on the exam answered the item correctly and all of the examinees who scored below the median answered incorrectly. In such a situation upper = 1.00 and p lower = 0.00. As such, the value of the item discrimination index D is 1.00 and the item is said to be a perfect positive discriminator. Many would regard this outcome as ideal. It suggests that those who knew the material and were well-prepared passed the item while all others failed it.

Though it's not as unlikely as winning a million-dollar lottery, finding a perfect positive discriminator on an exam is relatively rare. Most psychometricians would say that items yielding positive discrimination index values of 0.30 and above are quite good discriminators and worthy of retention for future exams.

Finally, notice that the difficulty and discrimination are not independent. If all the students in both the upper and lower levels either pass or fail an item, there's nothing in the data to indicate whether the item itself was good or not. Indeed, the value of the item discrimination index will be maximized when only half of the test takers overall answer an item correctly; that is, when $p = 0.50$. Once again, the ideal situation is one in which the half who passed the item were students who all did well on the exam overall.

Does this mean that it is never appropriate to retain items on an exam that are passed by all examinees, or by none of the examinees? Not at all. There are many reasons to include at least some such items. Very easy items can reflect the fact that some relatively straightforward concepts were taught well and mastered by all students. Similarly, an instructor may choose to include some very difficult items on an exam to challenge even the best-prepared students. The instructor should simply be aware that neither of these types of items functions well to make discriminations among those taking the test

.Reliability:

Simply put, a reliable measuring instrument is one which gives you the same measurements when you repeatedly measure the same unchanged objects or events. We shall briefly discuss here methods of estimating an instrument's reliability. The theory underlying this discussion is that which is sometimes called "classical measurement theory." The foundations for this theory were developed by Charles Spearman (1904, "General Intelligence," objectively determined and measures. American Journal of Psychology, 15, 201-293).

If a measuring instrument were perfectly reliable, then it would have a perfect positive (r = +1) correlation with the true scores. If you measured an object or event twice, and the true scores did not change, then you would get the same measurement both times.

We theorize that our measurements contain **random error**, but that the mean error is zero. That is, some of our measurements have error that make them lower than the true scores, but others have errors that make them higher than the true scores, with the sum of the score-decreasing errors being equal to the sum of the score increasing errors. Accordingly, random error will not affect the mean of the measurements, but it will increase the variance of the measurements.

Our definition of reliability is,

$$r_{XX} = \frac{\sigma_T^2}{\sigma_M^2} = \frac{\sigma_T^2}{\sigma_T^2 + \sigma_E^2} = r_{TM}^2.$$ That is, reliability is the proportion of the variance in the measurement scores that is due to differences in the true scores rather than due to random error.

Please note that I have ignored **systematic (nonrandom) error**, optimistically assuming that it is zero or at least small. Systematic error arises when our instrument consistently measures something other than what it was designed to measure. For example, a test of political conservatism might mistakenly also measure personal stinginess.

Also note that I can never know what the reliability of an instrument (a test) is, because I cannot know what the true scores are. I can, however, **estimate reliability**.

Test-Retest Reliability: The most straightforward method of estimating reliability is to administer the test twice to the same set of subjects and then correlate the two measurements (that at Time 1 and that at Time 2). Pearson r is the index of correlation most often used in this context. If the test is reliable, and the subjects have not changed from Time 1 to Time 2, then we should get a high value of r. We would likely be satisfied if our value of r were at least .70 for instruments used in research, at least .80 (preferably .90 or higher) for instruments used in practical applications such as making psychiatric. We would also want the mean and standard deviation not to change appreciably from Time 1 to Time 2. On some tests, however, we would expect some increase in the mean due to practice effects.

Alternate/Parallel Forms Reliability: If there two or more forms of a test, we want to know that the two forms are equivalent (on means, standard deviations, and correlations with other measures) and highly correlated. The r between alternate forms can be used as an estimate of the tests' reliability.

Split-Half Reliability: It may be prohibitively expensive or inconvenient to administer a test twice to estimate its reliability. Also, practice effects or other changes between Time 1 and Time 2 might invalidate test-retest estimates of reliability. An alternative approach is to correlate scores on one random half of the items on the test with the scores on the other random half. That is, just divide the items up into two groups, compute each subject's score on the each half, and correlate the two sets of scores. This is like computing an alternate forms estimate of reliability after producing two alternate forms (split-halves) from a single test. We shall call this coefficient the **half-test reliability coefficient, r_{hh}**.

Spearman-Brown: One problem with the split-half reliability coefficient is that it is based on alternate forms that have only one-half the number of items that the full test has. Reducing the number of items on a test generally reduces it reliability coefficient. To get a better estimate of the reliability of the full test, we apply the Spearman-Brown correction, $r_{sb} = \dfrac{2r_{hh}}{1 + r_{hh}}$.

Cronbach's Coefficient Alpha: Another problem with the split-half method is that the reliability estimate obtained using one pair of random halves of the items is likely to differ from that obtained using another pair of random halves of the items. Which random half is the one we should use? One solution to this problem is to compute the Spearman-Brown corrected split-half reliability coefficient for every one of the possible split-halves and then find the mean of those coefficients. This mean is known as Cronbach's coefficient alpha.

Maximized Lambda4: H. G. Osburn (Coefficient alpha and related internal consistency reliability coefficients, *Psychological Methods*, 2000, *5*, 343-355) noted that coefficient alpha is a lower bound to the true reliability of a measuring instrument, and that it may seriously underestimate the true reliability. They used Monte Carlo techniques to study a variety of alternative methods of estimating reliability from internal consistency. Their conclusion was that maximized lambda4 was the most consistently accurate of the techniques.

λ_4 is the r_{sb} for one pair of split-halves of the instrument. To obtain maximized λ_4, one simply computes λ_4 for all possible split-halves and then selects the largest obtained value of λ_4. The problem is that the number of possible split halves is $\dfrac{.5(2n)!}{(n!)^2}$ for a test with $2n$ items. If there are only four or five items, this is tedious but not unreasonably difficult. If there are more than four or five items, computing maximized λ_4 is unreasonably difficulty, but it can be estimated.

Construct Validity

Simply put, the construct validity of an operationalization (a measurement or a manipulation) is the extent to which it really measures (or manipulates) what it claims to measure (or manipulate). When the dimension being measured is an abstract construct that is inferred from directly observable events, then we may speak of "construct validity."

Face Validity. An operationalization has face validity when others agree that it looks like it does measure or manipulate the construct of interest

Content Validity. Assume that we can detail the entire population of behavior (or other things) that an operationalization is supposed to capture. Now consider our operationalization to be a sample taken from that population. Our operationalization will have content validity to the extent that the sample is representative of the population. To measure content validity we can do our best to describe the population of interest and then ask experts (people who should know about the construct of interest) to judge how well representative our sample is of that population.

Criterion-Related Validity. Here we test the validity of our operationalization by seeing how it is related to other variables. Suppose that we have developed a test of statistics ability. We might employ the following types of criterion-related validity:

• **Concurrent Validity.** Are scores on our instrument strongly correlated with scores on other concurrent variables (variables that are measured at the same time). For our example, we should be able to show that students who just finished a stats course score higher than those who have never taken a stats course. Also, we should be able to show a strong correlation between score on our test and students' current level of performance in a stats class.

• **Predictive Validity.** Can our instrument predict future performance on an activity that is related to the construct we are measuring? For our example, is there a strong correlation between scores on our test and subsequent performance of employees in an occupation that requires the use of statistics.

• **Convergent Validity.** Is our instrument well correlated with measures of other constructs to which it should, theoretically, be related? For our example, we might expect scores on our test to be well correlated with tests of logical thinking, abstract reasoning, verbal ability, and, to a lesser extent, mathematical ability.

Discriminant Validity. Is our instrument not well correlated with measures of other constructs to which it should not be related?

Relationship between reliability and validity:
If a test is unreliable, it cannot be valid. For a test to be valid, it must reliable. However, just because a test is reliable does not mean it will be valid. Reliability is a necessary but not sufficient condition for validity!

Standardization and norms: Scores on most psychological tests rarely provide absolute measures of the construct being assessed (e.g., self-esteem). Rather, tests frequently indicate the relative performance of a respondent when compared to others. Thus, most popular psychological tests are standardized, which means that there are fixed procedures for administration and scoring and that the test has been given to many different people in order to establish statistical norms for age, sex, race, and so on. Norms provide standards for interpreting test scores, so that a person's responses can be compared to an appropriate reference group. Without standardization and norms, it would be impossible to determine if an older adult's score is typical, above average, or below average, making the assessment worthless.

CHAPTER - 5
EVALUATION OF TEACHING

The Planning-Evaluation Cycle

Often, evaluation is construed as part of a larger managerial or administrative process. Sometimes this is referred to as the planning-evaluation cycle. The distinctions between planning and evaluation are not always clear; this cycle is described in many different ways with various phases claimed by both planners and

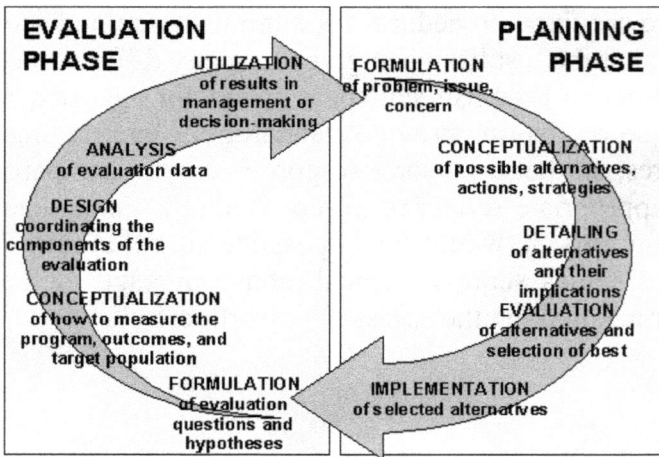

evaluators. Usually, the first stage of such a cycle -- the planning phase -- is designed to elaborate a set of potential actions, programs, or technologies, and select the best for implementation. Depending on the organization and the problem being addressed, a planning process could involve any or all of these stages: the formulation of the problem, issue, or concern; the broad conceptualization of the major alternatives that might be considered; the detailing of these alternatives and their potential implications; the evaluation of the alternatives and the selection of the best one; and the implementation of the selected alternative. Although these stages are traditionally considered planning, there is a lot of evaluation work involved. Evaluators are trained in needs assessment, they use methodologies -- like the concept mapping one presented later -- that help in conceptualization and detailing, and they have the skills to help assess alternatives and make a choice of the best one.

The evaluation phase also involves a sequence of stages that typically includes: the formulation of the major objectives, goals, and hypotheses of the program or technology; the conceptualization and operationalization of the major components of the evaluation -- the program, participants, setting, and measures; the design of the evaluation, detailing how these components will be coordinated; the analysis of the information, both qualitative and quantitative; and the utilization of the evaluation results.

Different modes of evaluation:
Let us begin with some of the different modes of evaluation, and some of the key terms used when describing the evaluation process.

Formative and summative evaluation:
Probably the most basic distinction is that between formative evaluation and summative evaluation.

Formative evaluation: This is evaluation that is carried out while a course, curriculum, educational package, etc is actually being developed, its main purpose being to find out whether it needs to be, and if so, whether it realistically can be improved. The key feature of all such evaluation is that it is designed to bring about improvement of the course, curriculum or educational package while it is still possible to do so, i.e. while the material has not yet been put into its operational form. In the case of a major course that is to be run throughout a country or internationally, such evaluation must clearly be carried out before the course design is finalized, the necessary resource materials mass produced, and the course implemented. In the case of an educational package, it must be carried out before the final package is published.

Summative evaluation: This is evaluation that is carried out once the development phase of a course, curriculum, educational package, etc has been completed, and the course curriculum or package is ready to use in its final form. The object of such evaluation is to determine whether it meets its design criteria, i.e. whether it does the job for which it was designed. Summative evaluation may also be carried out in order to compare one course, curriculum, educational package, etc with another (or several others), e.g. to compare the relative effectiveness of two different courses in the same general area, or to determine which of a number of different textbooks is most suitable for use in a particular course. In such evaluation, the object is not to improve the courses or textbooks being evaluated; rather, it is to choose between them.

External and internal evaluation
It is also possible to distinguish between external evaluation and internal evaluation.

External evaluation: This is evaluation that is carried out by someone who is (or was) not directly involved in the development or operation of the system being evaluated, i.e. by someone from out with the project team. Clearly, such an external evaluator has a number of advantages, bringing (it is to be hoped) objectivity, lack of vested interest, and the ability to look at matters from a fresh perspective. An external evaluator also has a number of disadvantages, however, most of which are related to relative value systems and to the lack of involvement the evaluator has had in project-related decisions. Such an evaluator may not, for example, fully appreciate why the development team chose to act in a particular way, or appreciate the thinking that lay behind certain decisions. The project team may also feel threatened by the evaluator, and feel that alien values or a negative, 'nit-picking' approach are being adopted.

Internal evaluation: This is evaluation that is carried out by someone from the actual project team. Clearly, such an evaluator has the advantage of understanding fully the thinking behind the development, together with an appreciation of any problems that may have arisen, and should also command the trust and cooperation of the other members of the team. On the other hand, such an evaluator may find it difficult to make any criticisms of the work carried out, and, because of their close involvement with the project, may be unable to suggest any innovative solutions to such problems that are identified. Such an internal evaluator will know only too well how the members of the group have struggled to produce their course, curriculum or package, and may shrink from the thought of involving them in more work.

Scientific and illuminative evaluation

Finally, let us examine the difference between the two main approaches that can be adopted to evaluation - the so-called 'scientific' (or agricultural/botanical) approach, and the 'illuminative' (or social/anthropological) approach.

Scientific evaluation: This has its origins in scientific experiments set up to assess the effects of specific variables (the nature of the soil, fertilizers, etc) on the growth of crops. Such experiments have tight controls, and the resulting outcomes can generally be measured relatively easily. When applied to education, the scientific approach has led to the use of systematic, objectives-oriented evaluation procedures. This 'traditional' strategy sets out to measure the extent to which a given instructional system has achieved certain specific goals (its objectives/learning outcomes) in relation to the students' pre-knowledge or existing skills. To this extent, the agricultural/botanical evaluation paradigm measures output against input, and often treats the differences statistically (click here for an example). Other factors in the system, such as the learning environment, teaching personnel, course content and structure, and teaching methods normally receive only incidental examination, if they are considered at all.

Illuminative evaluation: By comparison, the illuminative approach is more concerned with studying the on-going process of education. In general, the techniques used are far more subjective, and often involve personal value judgments of the results. The arguments in favour of this type of approach are that the variables in educational developments cannot be readily identified or controlled, and that 'inputs' and 'outputs' can be varied, complex, difficult to specify with certainty, and often virtually impossible to measure. In such cases, the evaluator explores the perceptions, opinions and attitudes of staff and students, using a variety of methods, in an attempt to reveal what was otherwise hidden in the educational process (click here for an example). The evaluation process is generally not rigidly structured or constrained, and usually gives the evaluator scope to follow up specific areas of interest as and when they become apparent. Illuminative evaluation of this kind has often been referred to as 'attempting to open up the black box of the educational process'.

Clearly, the mode of evaluation that is generally carried out within the context of the systems approach to course or curriculum design illustrated in Figure 1 is, by definition, formative evaluation, since the system is never regarded as being perfect or complete. Such evaluation will also normally be carried out internally, by the staff actually involved in developing and running the course or curriculum. It will generally also involve an approach that is largely illuminative, although it will probably also employ 'scientific' methods. Let us now examine a powerful theoretical model that can be used as the basis of all evaluation of this type.

Evaluation in Teaching Learning Process:
The Learning Environment:
The learning environment must respond to and respect a variety of learners' needs and abilities and be conducive to the incorporation of a range of strategies that encourage and support learning. Such an environment

• accommodates diversity in students' backgrounds, learning styles, personal assets and abilities

• fosters the involvement of students in meaningful learning activities

• supports the effective use of a wide range of resources, including technology and the media

• allows for active, interactive and collaborative learning

• is respectful of and fosters respect for divergent views, values and beliefs

• supports research and inquiry, evidence-based decision making, and planning and evaluation

• encourages and fosters learner responsibility and accountability for demonstrating stated learning outcomes. The classroom environment is critical to personal and social skill building. An atmosphere that recognizes and supports individual differences, that enhances self-esteem and that encourages differing opinions will encourage students to share and participate in learning activities. An open, supportive environment fosters a sense of security, belonging, respect, caring, worth and efficacy. Teachers should concentrate on establishing an atmosphere which invites student interaction, is respectful of the feelings, ideas and opinions of others and can be described as caring, collaborative and supportive. A way to facilitate this is to use activities which allow students to get to know each other, are non-threatening and enjoyable.

Role of the Teacher: Consideration needs to be given to the setup and organization of the physical space to foster individual and small group work, engage in some activities anonymously, display ongoing projects and finished work, accommodate learning centers and encourage creativity. The teacher plays a critical role in structuring and managing an effective and efficient learning environment. The primary role of the teacher is to guide and facilitate learning and to assist students with the acquisition of the skills and abilities required to demonstrate outcomes.

In contributing to the learning process, the teacher can

• assist students in the attainment of skills and abilities that enable them to take responsibility for and make reasoned decisions about food as it relates to health

• provide direction and encouragement to students as they engage in individual and collaborative learning activities

• act as a mentor and as a resource person as students make decisions about their own learning and the kinds of activities that will assist them in that process

• recognize and plan for diversity in students' backgrounds, learning styles, personal assets and abilities

• gage students' awareness of issues related to nutrition and assist them to build on this awareness

• help students establish and negotiate codes of conduct regarding individual and group behaviours that promote learning

• help students set limits and establish parameters for individual, class and lab behaviour

• provide opportunities to integrate knowledge, skills, attitudes and behaviours related to nutrition and health and to life-long learning

• record and report on student progress

Role of the Student The student plays a critical role in contributing to an effective and efficient learning environment and to the achievement of learning outcomes. The primary role of the student is to take responsibility for learning and to demonstrate achievement of curriculum outcomes. Students can

• strive to acquire skills and abilities that enable them to take responsibility for and make reasoned decisions

• build on knowledge and awareness of issues related to personal and family nutrition

• engage in learning activities that support personal learning styles and incorporate personal assets and abilities

• respect and contribute to a learning environment that supports diverse values, beliefs and opinions

• engage in individual and collaborative learning activities aimed at achieving course outcomes

• work with others to establish and employ codes of conduct regarding individual and group behaviours that promote learning

• respect the set limits and established parameters for individual and class, and lab behaviour

• engage in opportunities to integrate knowledge, skills, attitudes and behaviours related to personal and family nutrition

• take responsibility for directing their own learning, completing tasks and monitoring progress

• evaluate their progress and develop new strategies and plans for continuous learning and improvement

VARIOUS TECHNIQUES

Self-reporting techniques:

Self-reporting techniques of evaluation are those

techniques which are used in evaluation. To find out the reaction, of the respondents (students) to items concerning their characteristics or behaviour. The students generally are required to express their likes, dislikes, fears, hopes, ideas about religious beliefs etc. Their expressions reflect the way in which they cope with their own needs and demands of the environment they encounter with.

Significance of Self-reporting Techniques. Broadly speaking, self-reporting techniques are commonly used for measuring, the following traits of the students:

(1)   Adjustment
(2)   Attitude
(3)   Interest
(4)   Personality
(5)   Diverse traits

Examples of Self-reporting Techniques. These are as under:

(a)   Check list
(b)   Questionnaire
(c)   Rating scale.

Important Self-reporting Instruments: These are:

(1) Edward's Personal Preference Schedule
(2) The Minnesota Multi-phases Personality Inventory (MMPI)
(3) Minnesota Teacher Attitude Inventory (MTAI)
(4) Wood worth Personal Datasheet

Self-reporting techniques which come under the category of subjective techniques provide useful means for extracting the hidden treasure of students, acquired accumulated complex behaviour patterns of personality which are very difficult to discover through other devices. The information obtained through self reporting techniques may be collaborated suitably with information obtained through other techniques.

Limitations
i.   Being subjective in nature they are likely to have a biased element.
ii.   The respondents may attempt to present themselves as most favorable by giving fake or untrue responses.

The Precautions
(1)   After rearranging the items, techniques may be again used to find responses of the students after a short-interval.
(2)   'Lie' scales may be used to check receiving tendency,
(3)   'Forced Second Technique' may be used in which a student is given a choice to be exercised for performance which appears to be equally good or bad, e.g. who has exercised greater influence in developing your value system-your mother or father ?
(4)   Information obtained through self reporting techniques may be supplemented to the information obtained through other means.
(5)   More than one self-reporting technique may be used.
(6)   Norms for local population may be established.
(7)   Standardized inventories should be used.
(8)   Only due faith should be placed in this type of technique.

(9)   Only those techniques should be used in which the teacher has received reasonable amount of training.

(10)   In administering and interpreting the information, help of trained professionals may be obtained.

Observation:

Observation is one of the oldest techniques that man has made use of. Even today it is our common experience to notice that farmers feel the breeze, watch the sky, sun, moon and stars, all to determine what the weather is likely to be and what season is approaching.

The physicians and the psychologists depend heavily on what they observe of the patient's talk, gestures and facial expressions. Rousseau wrote, "Watch nature long and observe your pupil carefully before you say a word to him". Observation has been defined as, "measurement without instruments." In education, observation is the most commonly employed of all measurement techniques. In the present as well as in the past, students have been labeled as good, fair or poor in achievement and lazy or diligent in study etc., on the basis of observation. Similarly, teachers have listened to speeches and ranked students 1, 2, 3 and so on.

The subjective element is very predominant in observation. To eliminate the subjective element, reliance should be placed on a large number of individual observations or on the observations made by a large number of observers.

Behaviour is a reflection of personality. It must be observed very carefully, intelligently and scientifically as observation of behaviour has been recognized as basic to other techniques.

Merits

1. Being a record of the actual behaviour of the child, it is: none reliable and objective.
2. It is a study of an individual in a natural situation and is therefore more useful than the restricted study in a test situation.
3. This method can be used with children of all ages; of course, the younger the child, the easier it is to observe him. This method has been found very useful with shy children.
4. It can be used with a little training and almost all teachers can use it. It does not require any special tools or equipment.
5. It can be used in every situation.
6. It is adaptable both to individuals and groups.

Demerits

1. There is a great scope for personal prejudices and of the observer.
2. Records may not be written with hundred per cent accuracy as the observation is recorded after the actions of the observed. There is some time-lag.
3. The observer may get only a small sample of student behaviour. It is very difficult to observe everything that a student does or says. As far as possible, observations should be collected from several teachers.
4. It reveals the overt behaviour only-behaviour that is expressed and not that is within.

Requisites of Good Observation

As a research tool good observation is based on:

I.   Proper planning.
II.   Proper execution.
III.   Proper recording.
IV.   Proper interpretation.

Proper Planning of Observation

1.   Specific activities or units of behaviour to be observed must be clearly defined.
2.   An appropriate group of subjects be selected to observe.
3.   Scope of observation-whether individual or group should be decided.
4.   The length of each observation period, in umber of periods and interval between periods should be decided.
5.   The form of recording should be determined.
6.   The instruments to be used should be decided.
7.   Physical position of the observer. I should be demarcated.
8.   Proper tools for recording observation should be kept handy.
9.   Various terms may be studied.
        Proper Execution of Observation
An expert execution demands skill and resourcefulness on the part of the investigators. This depends upon.

I.   Proper arrangement of special conditions, or the subjects.
II.   Assuring proper physical position for observing.
III.   Focusing attention on the units of behaviour or the specific activities under observation.

IV.   Observing discreetly the length and Nurnberg, of periods and intervals decided upon.
V.   Proper handling of the recording instrument being used.
VI.   Utilizing well the training received in terms of expertness.

Devices Used in Observation are
I.   Check lists,
II.   Rating scale.
III.   Score cards:
IV.   Blank form of tally frequencies.

Recording of Observation
Generally two methods are employed for recording observation. This of the two methods to use depends upon the nature of the activities or behaviour of the group to be observed. The skill of the observer also plays an important role in deciding upon the method.
The first method is to record the observation simultaneously. It is useful in the sense that a time-gap may distort facts. However, at times, this may not be feasible when the action or activity performed is very swift. Moreover, this is likely to distract the subjects.
Facts may be recorded soon after the observation is over. This is helpful as this does not distract the mind of the subjects. The investigator may not be able to recall facts accurately after the interval of a few minutes.

Properper Interpretation
Records of observation should be interpreted cautiously and judiciously after taking into consideration various

limitations of planning and processes etc. involved in observation.

Recording Devices of Observation. Following are the major devices of observation:
(1)   Checklists.
(2)   Rating Scales.
(3)   Score Cards.

Planning Good, Reliable and Effective Observation
1.   Sampling to be observed should be adequate.
2.   Traits to be observed should be defined as accurately as possible.
3.   Methods recording should be simplified.
4.   Too Many variables may not be observed at a time.
5.   Length of' observation should be adequate.
6.   Length of observation period interval between period and, number of periods should be clearly stated
7.   Conditions of observation should remain constant.
8.   Observers should be fully equipped.
9.   Interpretations should be carefully made.

Essentials of a Good Observer
1.   Alertness.
2.   Ability IQ discriminates.
3.   Freedom. From-preconception.
4.   Emotional balance.

5.   Good eyesight.
6.   Right perception.
7.   Good speed of' recording.
8.   Ability to sift fact from fiction.

CHAPTER - 6
STATISTICAL SIGNIFICANE OF MEASURES OBTAINED

Here some important concept of statistics discussed below.

Important Formulas

$$Mean = \frac{\text{Sum of All the Scores}}{\text{Number of Scores}}$$

Standard Deviation

$$\text{Deviation Score Formula} = \sqrt{\frac{\sum (X - M)}{N-1}}$$

$$\text{Raw Score Formula} = \sqrt{\frac{N\sum X^2 - \left(\sum X\right)}{N(N-1)}}$$

Scaled Scores:

The **raw score** is an untransformed score from a measurement.

Raw Data

Statistical data in its original form, before any statistical techniques are used to refine, process, or summarize.

For Ex. When a person gets 85 answers correct on a 100 item test, the raw score= 85.

Is 85/100 correct on an exam good? It depends on the **evaluation system**.

Raw scores are difficult to interpret without additional information.

"The curve" has preset percentage categories for evaluation.

For Ex. A score in the top 10% on an exam = an 'A'. It is a relative position to other test scores.

"The standard" has preset cutoffs (relative to cut off values).

For Ex. 100-90 points correct on an exam = an 'A'. With the standard you are up against a system, not each other.

Percentile

One of the division points between 100 equal-sized pieces of the population when the population is arranged in numerical order. The 78th percentile is the number such that 78% of the population is smaller and 22% of the population is larger.

The percentile is transformed from a raw score. It will give you a relative position, for example, 1 to 99. The numbers = the percentage of scores below your raw score.

Obtaining a percentile rank of 80 means that whatever your raw score was, 80% of the other raw scores were below yours.

Raw Score	Percentile
78	50
85	60
90	70

Both sides (the distance between the scores) need to be equal for a linear transformation. The big problem with percentiles is that they are not linear transformations from raw scores; hence they are called "non-linear".

Centimeter	Inch
2.54	1
5.08	2

These are linear transformations.

As one side changes the other changes in equal proportions.

Percentiles are great at a descriptive level.

Standard Scores are linear transformations.

Raw scores are transformed into standard scores.

Changing a raw score to a percentile score or **percentile rank**:

$$PR = \frac{(Ra - .5)}{N} \times 100$$

PR = Percentile Rank

Ra = Rank of the raw score to be converted.

N = # of scores

Given a set of scores: 52, 89, 42, 13, 88, 76, 44, 45, 22, 105

Find the percentile rank (PR) for 45.

Rank all of the scores where the smallest value gets a rank of "1".

Score	13	22	42	44	45	52	76	88	89	105
Rank	1	2	3	4	5	6	7	8	9	10

$$Pr = \frac{(6 - \frac{1}{2})}{10} \times 100 = 55$$

PR for X = 88

$$Pr = \frac{(8 - \frac{1}{2})}{10} \times 100 = 75$$

Scaled Scores:

Percentile rank

Standard score (a linear transformation)

Z = raw score - mean of raw scores / standard deviation of raw scores

The Z score tells you how far the raw score is away from the mean in terms of standard deviation units. It does not change the shape of the distribution!

Raw score does not change into a **bell shaped curve** when changed into standard scores. The numbers do not change physically, the measurement just changes. It transforms the unit of measurement you are working with.

Percentile

Z score

mean of Z scores = 0

standard deviation of Z scores = 1

If the Z score is negative, this says that the raw score was below the mean of raw scores.

If the Z score is positive, this says that the raw score was above the mean of raw scores.

If the Z score is zero, this says that the raw score was equal to the mean of raw scores.

McCall T-Score Scale (Personality Tests)

The raw scores have been converted resulting in a scale where the mean = 50 and the standard deviation = 10.

Ex. Given the raw scores 22, 17, 19, 37, 26 convert 26 to a scaled score on the McCall T-Score Scale.

Ex. -23, 18, -2, 5, 44, 39, 19, 18. What is the percentile rank for a raw score of 18 (X= 18).

Tied Ranks are 2 numbers having the same values, for example '18' and '18'.

Rank	Scores
1	-23
2	-2
3	5
4	18
5	18
6	19
7	39
8	44

Look at ranks 4 and 5, take the mean of these = 4.5.

$$Pr = \frac{(4.5 - \frac{1}{2})}{8} \times 100 = 50$$

Ex. 4, 29, 17, 29, 29, 30, 7, 11, 14. Convert 29 to a percentile.

Rank	Scores
1	4
2	7
3	11
4	14
5	17
6	29
7	29
8	29
9	30

$$\text{PR for } X = 29 \quad Pr = \frac{(7 - \frac{1}{2})}{9} \times 100 = \frac{6.5}{9} \times 100 = 72$$

Dr. Urvashi may use different wording on your exams. Don't get confused. Percentile and Percentile Rank mean the same thing.

Ex. Convert 46 to a percentile rank.

X (raw scores)	Rank
100	7
80	6
29	2
46	5
18	1
45	4
34	3

1) Rank the numbers.

$$\text{PR for X} = 46 \quad Pr = \frac{(5 - \frac{1}{2})}{7} \times 100 = \frac{4.5}{7} \times 100 = 64.3 \approx 64$$

What does this mean?
It means that 64% of the scores lie below 46.

Ex. Convert 80 to a Z score.

$$Z = \frac{Score - \text{Mean of all Scores}}{\text{Std. Dev of All the Scores}} = \frac{X - M}{S}$$

Note: All stand deviation computations in this course uses N − 1 as the divisor.

$$S = \sqrt{\frac{\sum(X - M)}{N - 1}} \quad M = \text{Mean.}$$

M = Mean
X-bar is also used but not in this class because it can be confused with X which is a vector.

Convert 80 to a Z score.

1. Find the mean and standard deviation.
M = 50.285
SD = 27.154

Z = 80 - 50.28 / 27.154
Z = 1.094 = 1.09
This says that the score of 80 lies over 1 standard deviation above the mean (50.285).

The following is very important:
Percentiles are represented as integers.
Z scores are carried to 2 decimal places.
To insure accuracy at 2 decimal places you must carry to at least 3 decimal places in your calculations.

1. Find the Z score for 80.
2. Use the formula listed above.

$$100 (1.09) + 500 = 609.$$

Ex. Convert 80 to a McCall T- score scale.

T score = 10 (Z score for 80) + 50
$$10 (1.09) + 50 = 10.9 + 50 = 60.9.$$

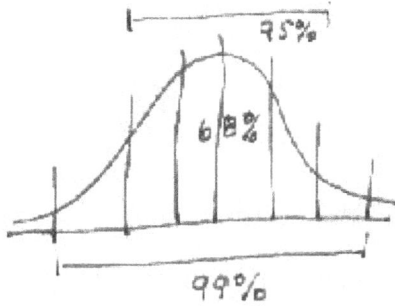

Ex. Convert X = 80 to a scaled score where the mean = 100 and standard deviation = 16.
Scaled score = 16 (Z score for 80) + 100
Scaled score = 16 (1.09) + 100 = 117.44.

CHAPTER - 7
USING THE RESULTS OF MEASUREMENT

Here discuss, probably the main purposes for which tests and other measuring instruments are used in the schools today. Certainly they seem important and worthy of careful consideration. It will be the aim of this chapter to discuss these purposes and to show how measurement can contribute to the attainment of each.

Basic to using the results of measurement is the interpretation of scores. A test score is merely a number, devoid of meaning in and by itself. Not until it is related to something does it become meaningful and thus useful. Before we proceed with a discussion of the various uses of test results, it would be well to take another look at a device which facilities interpretation.

Placement and Promotion

One of the primary uses of test results is placement of pupils at particular grade levels, promoting, accelerating, or holding them as may be judged appropriate. Ideally, pupils should be placed at levels where they can learn without being unduly discouraged, overworked, or bored.

Homogeneous Grouping

Recent years have seen a greatly increased emphasis on quality in education and greatly increased interest in providing stimulating and challenging opportunities for the superior pupil. It is felt that we have permitted the most able pupils to go along at "half speed" as it were, with a resultant loss of interest and accomplishment. Advocates of homogeneous grouping

81

believe that providing a more rewarding and challenging education for gifted pupils can be done more easily and successfully if such pupils are grouped or sectioned so that they can have an enriched programme and can also proceed at an accelerated pace. It is also maintained that homogeneous sections for slow learners are advantageous for them in that the instruction can proceed at a pace more suited to their abilities. Furthermore, it is felt that the slower learners in a class of similar capacity and interests avoid the discouragement and failure that are often their lot when they are instructed in classes with pupils who are much more able academically.

Diagnosis and Remedial Work: The purpose of a diagnostic test is to find the specific weaknesses and strengths of a pupil in a particular area of study or subject-matter.

Counseling and Guidance

Broadly stated, the function of the counselor or guidance worker is to help pupils achieve satisfactory and satisfying solutions to their problems

Marking:

Every teacher has the responsibility for making the best judgments he can about his pupils' achievement and development in subject-matter, maturity, citizenship, character, and other areas. These judgments may be expressed in various ways, but marks are the most common. As our schools and educational programmes are constituted, marks are an integral part of the system. Pupils, parents and administrators expect them. They are the terms in which appraisals of a pupil's accomplishments are communicated. It is, therefore, only sensible for the teacher to try to do the best possible job of evaluating and marking, to strive constantly to improve the marking system, and to do his best to keep abreast of improvements in marking practices. It is generally agreed that marks should be assigned on a comparative basis. Letter marks have several advantages they are easier to use, easier to interpret, and are more realistic. Marks should be based as much as possible on objective measurements. As far as possible, marks should express accomplishment of specific goals rather than the results of global or omnibus appraisal.

Curriculum evaluation

The curriculum evaluator works in two major areas. First, he tries to evaluate a course or programme as it unfolds or proceeds. Thus, he may find by tests or other means that instruction in fractions is not producing the results desired and he therefore tries to find better methods of instruction. Second, curriculum evaluation may focus on the end product to determine the effectiveness of the course of instruction as a whole. As an example, the evaluator may try to determine by various means how well-prepared graduates of a nurse's course in psychology apply its principles in their relationships to patients.

Performance and contracting

At this point it seems appropriate to mention an innovation known as performance contracting. Briefly, this refers to a plan whereby private firms are employed by a school board to come into a school or district to take over teaching a basic subject like reading or -arithmetic, usually to disadvantaged children. The terms of the contract specify that the contractor will be paid according to the "amount of learning" he is able to produce in a given time such as one school year. The funds in most instances come from some federal agency.

Motivational

It is a generally accepted principle of psychology that the practice of a skill with knowledge of results-that is, of errors, successes, and over-all improvement-produces much more progress than practice wherein such information is withheld from the learner.

Identification and Study of Exceptional Children

Children with obvious physical handicaps such as those who are crippled, those having nervous disorders as a result of brain damage, and the like, pose little problem as far as identification is concerned. The exact nature of the disability will be diagnosed and treatment prescribed by medical means.

BIBLIOGRAPHY

Alexander, s., & Hedberg, j. (1994). Evaluating technology-based learning: which model? In K. Beattie, C. McNaught & S. Wills (Eds.), Multimedia in higher education: Designing for change in teaching and learning (pp. 233-244). Amsterdam: Elsevier.

Asthana B.B. and Asthana S. (2007). Measurement and Evaluation in Psychology and Education.Agra :Vinod Pustak Mandir.

Bhargav M. (1999).Psychological Test and Measurement.Agra:Seguin Form Board.

Bloom, B.S. (Ed.). Engelhart, M.D., Furst, E.J., Hill, W.H., Krathwohl, D.R. (1956). Taxonomy of Educational Objectives, Handbook I: The Cognitive Domain. New York: David McKay Co Inc.

Blumberg, P., Alschuler, M. D., & Rezmovic, V. (1982). Should taxonomic leels be considered in developing examinations? Educational and Psychological Measterment, 42, 1-7.

Cruz, E. (2004). Encyclopedia of Educational Technology: Bloom's Revised Taxonomy.

Ebel, R. L. & Frisibie, D. A (1991). Essentials of Educational Measurement (5th Edition). New Delhi: PHI.

Fisher, W. (2010). IRT and confusion about Rasch measurement. Rasch Measurement Transactions, 24, 1288.Retrieved romhttp://www.rasch.org/rmt.

Forehand, M. (2005). Bloom's taxonomy: Original and revised. In M. Orey (Ed.), Emerging perspectives on learning, teaching, and technology.

Goswami, Marami (2003). Measurement and Evaluation in Education and Psychology. Guwahati: Armag Printers.

Gronlund N. E. (1976). Measurement and evaluation in teaching. New York: Macmillan Publishing Company Inc.

Linn R. L. & Gronlund N. E. (2003). Measurement and assessment in teaching 8th ed. New Delhi: Pearson Education (Singapore) Pte. Ltd.

Kottke, J. L., & Schuster, D. J (1990). Developing tests for measuring Bloom's learning outcomes. Psychological Reports, 66, 27-32.

Kubiszyn, T., & Borich, G. (2004). Educational Testing and Measurement: Classroom Application and Practice (7th ed.). India : John Wiley & Sons, Inc.

Kunen, S., Cohen, R., & Solman, R. (1981). Levels-of-processing analysis of Bloom's taxonomy. Journal of Educational Psychology, 73, 202-211.

Pandey, K.P(2011).Educational Measurement of Evaluation. Varanasi:Vishwaridyalya Prakashan.

Reynolds, C. R. et.al. (2009). Measurement and Assessment in Education. 2nd ed. New Delhi: PHI learning Pvt. Ltd.

Scriven, M. (1967). The methodology of evaluation. In R. W. Tyler, R. M. Gagne, & M. Scriven (Eds.), *Perspectives of curriculum evaluation*, 39-83. Chicago, IL: Rand McNally.

Simon, N. (2000). Managing the CI department: Cognition and performance. Competitive Intelligence Magazine, 3, 53-56.

Saettler, Paul (1990). *The Evolution of American Educational Technology*. Englewood, Colorado: Libraries Unlimited, Inc., p. 350.

Thorndike R. M. (2011). Measurement and Evaluation in Psychology and Education (8th Edition). New Delhi: PHJ.

www.ingramcontent.com/pod-product-compliance
Lightning Source LLC
Chambersburg PA
CBHW060404050426
42449CB00009B/1890